T0104887

Confidance

A COLLECTION
OF POEMS

DR. STELLA NOWICKI

Order this book online at www.trafford.com
or email orders@trafford.com

Most Trafford titles are also available at major online book retailers.

Print information available on the last page.

ISBN: 978-1-4669-3319-4 (sc)
ISBN: 978-1-4669-3320-0 (e)

Trafford rev. 12/09/2016

 www.trafford.com

North America & international
toll-free: 1 888 232 4444 (USA & Canada)
fax: 812 355 4082

Dedicated to People
who love people

Contents

Acknowledgements...xi

About the Book..xiii

The Secret of Life 1

Tango..2

Ode to Freedom 4

Emptiness...6

Forbidden colors of nude 8

For the first time 10

Universal Happiness...13

Just Laugh...15

Sweet Surprise 16

Nobody's Child 17

Kindness 18

I've Had Enough 19

Surrealism of Colors..20

In a Broken Box of Rules and Laws 23

Perhaps It's True..25

Men are from Mars 28

Between "Momento" and Sacramento 30

Anything For A Rush...32

Time For Love 33

Creativity 34

Unrealistic Wish? 35
Simplicity of Mind 37
Surrealistic Vision 39
Just Believe Me..41
Find The Wings 42
Agreement...43
I Want To Be With You 44
Mirage of Happiness 46
Puzzle of Life..47
A Gift From My Heart...48
Christmas List...49
Untreated Disease 50
Unconditional Love...52
Unjealous Woman 53
Music Everywhere 54
Life Before Year 2000..56
Computer In Space 57
Why?..59
What Can I Give You...60
Angels Do Not Survive 61
Nothing Is Crazy 63
Forbidden.. 64
Miracle...65
A Realist...66
Hopeless...67
I Do 68
Erotic Dream 69
Rock me...70
Midlife Crises..71
Spoil Me...72
Sometimes..73
Would You Hear? 75

Between Dark and Dusk 76
Soul Full Of Flowers 78
A Plethora Of Poems 79
The Notebook 80

Photos

Portrait of Stella Nowicki painted by her Husband.....82
Stella and Bogdan Nowicki 83
Stella Nowicki medical school graduation photo 84
My 2 daughters Natalie(left) and Joanna(right bottom)
My son Alex(middle), my husband Bogdan(Back),
my granddaughter Isabelle(in joanna's arms), and
me(right) 85
Stella at home...86
Isabelle 87
Joanna and Isabelle...88
Natalie Alex Joanna Christmas Picture.....................89
Stella and Bogdan Dancing 90
Stella in the Lab 91
About the Author 93

Acknowledgements

I would like to thank my children Alexander Nowicki and Natalie Nowicki for finding time during their busy medical school schedules to help edit my work, and for "Polishing" my English. I would also love to thank my wonderful husband Bogdan and my children: Natalie, Alex, Joanna and Isabelle (Joanna's daughter) for loving and supporting me every day.

About the Book

"Confidance" is a provocative and original book of poetry where facts and feelings are imaginarily integrated in to the romance of reality and the drama of surrealism.

There are about 55 poems written by Dr. Stella Nowicki a poet, scientist, philosopher; a women with soul, vision and wisdom. She changed the theme of traditional poetry into a powerful passionate engaging storyteller of spiritual life. These prolific, humorous poems make you smile and realize that life is a roller-coaster filled with a plethora of extraordinary experiences, touching your soul with the music of your imagination.

These insightful poems full of metaphor and analogy, punctuated by quotes from famous people are published to inspire healing thoughts and positively impact people who aren't afraid of taking chances and critics.

It doesn't take much to criticize and point out mistakes. It takes wisdom, soul, and confidance to provide the vision where mistakes become the seeds of new opportunity.

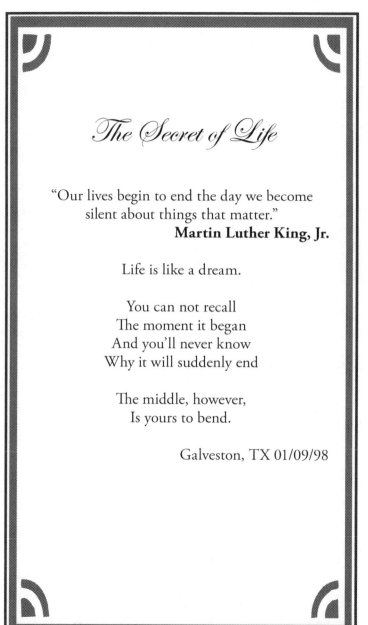

The Secret of Life

"Our lives begin to end the day we become
silent about things that matter."
Martin Luther King, Jr.

Life is like a dream.

You can not recall
The moment it began
And you'll never know
Why it will suddenly end

The middle, however,
Is yours to bend.

Galveston, TX 01/09/98

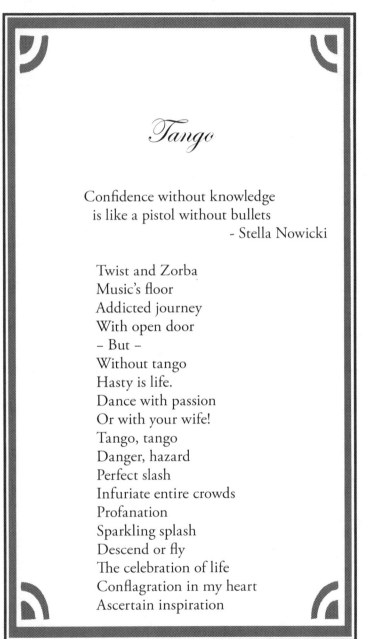

Tango

Confidence without knowledge
is like a pistol without bullets
- Stella Nowicki

Twist and Zorba
Music's floor
Addicted journey
With open door
– But –
Without tango
Hasty is life.
Dance with passion
Or with your wife!
Tango, tango
Danger, hazard
Perfect slash
Infuriate entire crowds
Profanation
Sparkling splash
Descend or fly
The celebration of life
Conflagration in my heart
Ascertain inspiration

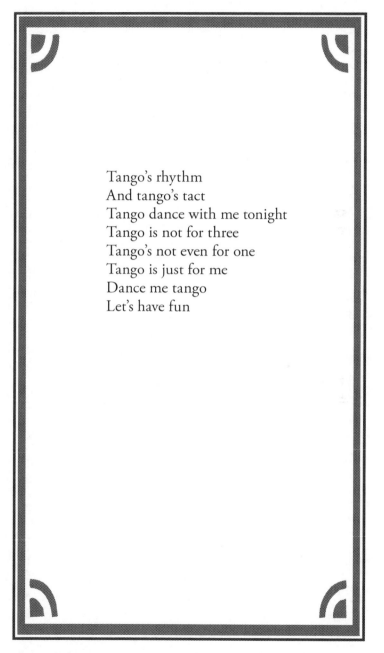

Tango's rhythm
And tango's tact
Tango dance with me tonight
Tango is not for three
Tango's not even for one
Tango is just for me
Dance me tango
Let's have fun

Ode to Freedom

"Freedom consists not in doing what we like, but
in having the right to do what we ought."
- Pope John Paul II

Play with the orchestra,
First violin,

Feel like a maestro -
This is my dream.

Drink a bee's honey,
Live in the flowers,
Don't count money,
Don't count hours.

Kissing a tiger
On his big lips.
Be a part of the jungle
Swing on tree tops,

Dance with a bear
All year round

Until in the forest
The first snow's on the ground.

Is this what you want?
Then you can try
Don't stop, just go!
Someone, survive.

Galveston, TX, USA

Emptiness

Empty love
Empty spot
Empty night
Empty day
Empty bed
Empty plate
Empty dream
Empty tear
Don't cry baby, don't cry
Nothing is forever, even pain
Empty glass
Empty trust
Empty book
Empty look
Empty mind
Only heart, Full of love
Only moon
Only sky
Full of stars
And beliefs
Full of hope
Empty hope

Empty spell
Empty bell
Empty crowd
Empty dress
Empty dance
Empty rest

Empty speech;
Empty beach, Out of season
Empty feel
Full of guilt
Empty song
Empty life
Let's go in
Let's go out
Nothing helps, Empty try

Emptiness

Galveston, TX '98

Forbidden colors of nude

"Colors like features follow the changes
of the emotions."
- Pablo Picasso.

Forbiden colors of nude,
Add to your waves,
Gray Color, "Broken Color"

Oh yes, even colors are broken.

When they slightly gray,
Are they artistically incompatible?
Or just simply gray?
Bristle brushes smoothly run
Threatened fingers, tracing down

In the background, viridian green
Cobalt Blue makes eyes of dreams.

Cadmium yellow, discreet light
Shape the figure during night.

The geometric shape of hands
shrouds the triangle 'tween the hips.
The golden shadow of her breast
And two legs in arrest.

Basic movements to reflect
Alabaster sheets floating to the bed.
Broken colors, embarrassed gaze
As the artist sees her
Through the morning haze

For the first time

"Neither a lofty degree of intelligence nor imagination nor both together go to the making of genius. Love, love, love, that is the soul of genius."

Wolfgang Amadeus Mozart

First look, first smile
First touch, first goodbye
First rendezvous, first kiss
First love with meaning

First agreement full of secrets
First disappointment felt
Deep emptiness. It's over
Everything is meaningless

No love, no hope, no colors
Only skys full of red
Only hearts full of pain

Until . . . .
First smile, first laugh
First look so deep
First touch—distrust

First glass of wine
First dance, first hug
First time without love
First kiss, so nice

First charm to avoid

No love, new hope—first time
First color of soul
First impulse of existence

First love, real love
Forever, first scare
To lose your mind
To lose yourself

For the first time.

Universal Happiness

"It is not living that matters,
but living rightly"

- Socrates

Energy derived from the sun
Is converted to happiness
By cordial transcriptions in my heart
Why?
Because, I love my planet
And the solar constellations
This… makes me happy forever

Do you love your stars and planet?

My planet? No, I don't have one

Oh no, I feel sorry for you
No love... no happiness... only pain…

I would be unhappy as well
Totally worthless, Oh yes!

You know, I have an idea
I can share my planet with you.

Oh no! I will feel like a stranger.

Why?
Don't be afraid, it's not a danger.

You see, I don't believe in love

Then try to love and change beliefs.
This is the way to feel a part of the universe.
This is the way to find universal happiness.

Gdansk, 1999

Just Laugh

"There is more to life than
increasing its speed."
- Mahatma Gandhi

Don't worry,
Laugh, just laugh
It's good for you,
It's good for me
I like laughing faces.
Laugh, because
Only laughing could be real
In an artificial world.
Nothing is more important.
Laughter is a symbol of humanity,
A symbol of happiness.
Laughing is exclusively
A human expression.
Only our laugh distinguishes
Us from other creatures,
Then laugh
Whenever you can,
As long as you can
To prove your humanity.
14.08.98

Sweet Surprise

"There is nothing either good or bad
but thinking makes it so."
- William Shakespeare

Touch this? He asked
Not with a hand with a mouth
Yes like that.

Could you try?
One more time
Her eyes were sparkling
With light from her heart
Expressing ecstasies and happiness
Try one more time? He asked
She did

Her lips were sweet
He kissed them twice
Such a wonderful surprise
The power of taste
Only for lovers
With a box of chocolates
In a lovely place

Nobody's Child

"You gain strength, courage and confidence by every experience in which you stop to look fear in the face...you must do the thing you think you cannot do."

-Eleanor Roosevelt

I am nobody's child
I try my best to be happy
I try and then I am
Happy, Happy like that
As happy as can be,
Nobody's child.
The world is strange around me.
The crowd is strange outside
But I am happy, or I think I'm happy
I want to be happy
Happy?- nobody's nasty to me
No body Loves me, nobody kisses me
Nobody wants me, nobody screams at me
Nobody needs me, wait for me.
- Nobody's child.

Kindness

Kiss my tears and pray
That I will not lose my humanity
For all this, what you did to me
Your atavistic manners
Awake an anxious lion in me
For whom, you are
A peace of ordinary meat

Kiss my tears and pray
It's time to feed this wild lion
To satisfy his basic needs
To calm down his atavistic instinct.

Kiss my tears and pray
That I will be kind to your unkind animal
That I won't see you as anything less
Than an ordinary human being

03/06/98

I've Had Enough

Sometimes I have enough
Of fighting with everything,
With every bit of dust.
Sometimes I have enough
Of agreeing with everybody
And with time - that runs.
Sometimes I wish to stop
You, myself, and time.
Sometimes I wish to drop
You, my day and time.
Sometimes it's really not fun
To be where people are going.
Sometimes it's okay
To go where your soul is floating.
Sometimes it's good to know
That bad times come and go.
Sometimes time is gone
Before you noticed time at all.

04.06.98

Surrealism of Colors

"It is a man's own mind, not his enemy
or foe, that lures him to evil ways."
- Buddha

Orange of red.
Yellow of Light
On the ocean's bed.

A draining storm in the night
Fills the brain with dread

A contemporary picture
Of blue and white
With a sense of hell
crushes the light
As the scent of magnolia
Signals the end of time

After the rain
The Mission of time
covering hopelessness
And the pain of mine

Orange of red
Darkness of light
Only Love
Lets us survive

"I am tired to being a man"

"Wisdom begins in wonder."
Socrates

This is what Pablo Neruda said
I'm tired to being myself
But who else can I be
Who else?
I can be whoever I wish to be
This is what my father said to me
But, where to find the wish.

In a Broken Box of Rules and Laws

"Are we to paint what's on the face, what's
inside the face, or what's behind it?"
- Pablo Picasso

A perfectly round face
Shadowed by secret feelings
Perfectly matches
Your simple dreams
Between the nights
Between the willings
That may surprise
Your wild feelings

A broken box
Of rules and laws
Creates a sense of destiny
between generations
Without any meanings.

It tortures our nature
Spotless like a star
Perfectly round,
Cyclic like life

Perhaps It's True

Undressed heart
With ornaments
Extreme but, attractive
Volcano of needs for
The designer
To decorate
As you wish

Perhaps it's true

But who knows how?
No hugs, no clue

Then powerful paints
That colored even stone
With passion in my hands,
Somehow turn you on

In the soft light of the moon
I am so impressed
You look so beautiful
Such a success!
Your heart is dressed

Perhaps it's true
Unrehearsed spread
You let me do
Your lips are wet

Fulfill volcano
Of new heart dressed
With ornaments

Electric light
Speeding in your eyes
Shock for my mind

I am looking twice
Perhaps I'm wrong
Naïve picture
Undressed heart

Spendthrift art
I'm sure you know

You feel mad
You let me go
Laying on a bed
Mess in your mind
Afraid to dream
About real love

Men are from Mars

Women are from Venus
When he said no

She thought maybe
When she said maybe
He thought, maybe not
When he showed love
He thought forever
But he didn't tell her
So she heard never
He touched her face
She felt his sense
Because he is from Mars

She is from Venus

He affects by sunshine
She affects by moon
She wants to be loved
He wants to make love
She wants to drink

He wants to be drunk
She wants chocolate
He doesn't care
   She wants to have a baby

   He wants to be a baby for her
She wants a bedroom and hot tub
He wants a garage and workshop
She wants a shiny dress
He wants her undressed

   She has her menstrual cycle

   He wants a motorcycle
But hypothetically they can communicate
When they are in Love
Because of Einstein's Theory of Relativity

Between "Momento" and Sacramento

"The shortest story in history- Momento,
lamento, sacramento." – Unknown

I only wish
To own your heart, see your beauty

I could be your angel
Or act like a floozy

Just to be
Whatever you want from me

I could be your devil or your lord

I'd treat you in the most charming way
I'd be your sunshine on a rainy day,

Even your music in rock and roll,
Just for "momento" without "lamento"

But you only wish
To reach the pearls of "sacramento"

Conflagration in my heart
Ascertain inspiration
Tango's rhythm
And tango's tact

Tango dance with me tonight

Tango is not for three
Tango even not for one
Tango is just for me
Dance me tango
Let's have fun

Anything For A Rush

Grab my hand and kiss,
Or just simply caress.
I don't really care
Just do something now.
Don't ask why.
Don't ask, "may I?"
Help me feel
That you are here.
Grab my hand and touch.
Anything for a rush.
Make me realize
That I am alive.
I just want to know
If I'm right or wrong.
Even make me mad
I don't really care.
I don't want to feel death,
It's just not fair.
If this you cannot do
Than I leave you with my ghost
Because with you,
Of me, I've left most.

04.06.98

Time For Love

"Intelligence without ambition is a
bird without wings."
- Salvador Dali

I know you love me, sometimes,
When you have time,
Or maybe when I have time,
To feel that you love me.
Sometimes I don't even care
If your love is for me, there.
But sometimes it's just painful
That I am not your one most wonderful.
But sometimes it's wonderful
To feel that pain is a fool.
A fool like no one else
Killing your love and your time.
Because sometimes,
You spend too much time with your pain
……Sometimes it's good to have no time.

Creativity

"The poets are only the interpreters
of the Gods."

- Socrates

Creative mind
Of a lovely creature
Creates a love
For a better future.
Creative time
Do not arrive
Creature, feel dumb
Future is alive.
Life full of dreams.
No time, no tears.
Just creative beliefs
The past disappears.

11.08.98

Unrealistic Wish?

I want to touch you
Where no one can reach
I want to find my only place
–Not in your body,
–Not in your heart
I want this untouchable part

I want to meet your soul
I want to find what is below
I want you to be there
–Only with you
Just for a second
To find the truth

Give to me with passion
Without pain,
Without tears
Part of your Ego,

This,
What you couldn't years ago

11/ 18, 1997, Galveston, Texas

Simplicity of Mind

"Simplicity is the highest goal, achievable
when you have overcome all difficulties."
- Frederic Chopin

Oh no! Please stop
Why? Don't you enjoy?
Don't ask, just stop

Oh! Then let's talk
About unique recipes
To talk about food?
Oh no! I don't want
Why?
Because this
Makes me hungry

So what then we can eat
Oh no! I had my dinner already
Then let's talk about history
History? This subject makes me sleepy

So! What about politics?

Oh no! Don't make me angry
Than let's talk about music
About music? Okay

Only let me take my dancing shoes

Oh I see, now I understand
Why you didn't want
To talk about sex

01/11/98

Surrealistic Vision

Surrealistic Vision
Of real artist
Provoke my brain
For dual excitement

In storm of feelings
With hurricane disaster
I touch the causes
With dream of a master

Explosion of colors
Fusion of lights
Diminished dreams
Of sleepless minds

After the battle
Synchronized seduction
Translated signaling
To real action

For unknown future
Surrealistic vision
Have real past
Forever thrashed

Just Believe Me

I don't want to love you
I don't want to kiss you
I don't want to own you
I don't want to miss you

I don't want to remember
I don't want to harm you
Then what do I want?

Maybe I don't know
No! I do know
But, how to call this?
This I don't know

Find The Wings

I don't want to be your lover
I don't want to be your wife
I don't want to be your mother
I don't want to use your time

I just want to be your dream
Not all night, not all day
I just want to be between
For this touching, tender play

I can be your only queen
Let the wind sail this boat
Let yourself be a king
Let us fly on a moony road

To find your and my wings

Agreement

Give me a poem from your heart
Give me the beauty of your thoughts
Let me feel the tenderness of your lips
Give me the secrets of your dreams

Or give me a cup of coffee
Or maybe a glass of wine
Or give me just a glass of water
But only when you dim the lights

I Want To Be With You

Please, take me to your world
I will be there your soul
O! my dear
Soul is not useful there
Take me to your life
I will be there your wife
O! life is too crude
I can't be there with you

O my little man
Take me for today
Today I have a plan
Maybe another time
Take me to your dream
Please let me in
But dreams, I never own
You will be there alone
Then take me to your heart
I will be there your part

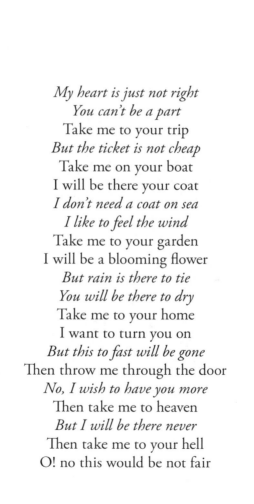

My heart is just not right
You can't be a part
Take me to your trip
But the ticket is not cheap
Take me on your boat
I will be there your coat
I don't need a coat on sea
I like to feel the wind
Take me to your garden
I will be a blooming flower
But rain is there to tie
You will be there to dry
Take me to your home
I want to turn you on
But this to fast will be gone
Then throw me through the door
No, I wish to have you more
Then take me to heaven
But I will be there never
Then take me to your hell
O! no this would be not fair

Mirage of Happiness

Dance me to the rest of your love
If you want to see me happy
Kiss me to the rest of your night
If you want to find a happy face
Touch me to the rest of your temptation
To discover happiness of soul
Love me to the rest of your dreams
To define what happiness means
Hug me for the rest of your dance
Want me to the last of your dusk
Paint me to the last of your rainbow
Trust me to the end of your voyage
To experience happiness
To our endless mirage

May 1998, Galveston, TX

Puzzle of Life

Temptation of dreams
Unpredictable power
Echo of whisper chills
Meaning of life
Ocean of beliefs
Flashlight of night
Puzzle of gifts
Bucket of facts
Prelude for dance
Music in tacts
Tunder of veins
Stones on your road
Glaring in your eyes
Promisess of God
Unexpected lies
Shaping endless chain
Of escaping days
Moon fully flame
Not worth the trade

A Gift From My Heart

I wish to give you
Blue of the sky
And pearls from the sea
Color of roses
Flashlight of stars
Diamonds of earth
Wind of my songs
Music of shell
For magic dance
Fragrance of spring
Beauty of life
Power of God
That only comes
With secrets
Of spiritual love

Christmas List

You ask me
What I want
This year
For Christmas Eve
I want only
A few things
Here you are -
My wish list:
A magic carpet
To take you there
That you would want
To stay
Forever with me
Forever for me
Forever every day
New diamonds
From your heart
And chocolate kisses
On the Christmas tree
This is my list by half
I wish to have
Snow by my door
Champagne in bathtub
And fire from your soul

Untreated Disease

Psychotherapy
A popular job
But there is no therapy
For an ill soul.

Psychologists
Psychiatrists
Busy
All the time,
But who could
Cure your
Broken heart?
A Cardiologist?
- Of course
They know
All about
Hearts, but
Even they
Could not repair
A broken heart
An ophthalmologist
Will fix your eyes....

You will see better.
For a pediatrician
You are too old
For a geriatric
You to young
Family doctor?
Familiar with everything
But these symptoms
Not for him

Gynecologist?
They don't touch
This part is over their mind
Pathologists may try
Forensics will not find
Then you can walk
Or - you can die
With a crushed soul
With a broken heart
Such a disease
Does not exist
Therefore undiagnosed
Therefore untreated

Unconditional Love

I love you
When rain is
Around you
I love you
When you are
In snow
I fall in love
When you are laughing
I fall in love
When you are jumping
I need you for dance
And for a dream
I love you
When you are polite
And even if you scream
I kiss you
When you are sleeping
I touch you
When you are not with me
You ask me
What I want to say?
Just that I love you
Anyway

Unjealous Woman

She was never jealous
Of any thing
Not of new diamond
Not of a new dress
Fancy cars or houses
She was never jealous
Of talent or money
Beauty or perfumes
But one day she saw her
Then suddenly she didn't feel well
Not because of her beauty
Not because of her job
She started to be jealous
Because he hugged her
And kissed her so deeply
Looking in her eyes
Like nobody else
Existed in time

Music Everywhere

Melody of wind
Melody of sea
Melody of your mind
When you talk to me

Music of guitars
Music of glasses
In crowded bars

Music of rain
Melody of hearts
The song of pain
The shadow in the dark

The echo of bells
From Christmas songs
Beauty of tears
From your lonely soul

Music everywhere
Sways the wedding dress
Unique Melodies
Wispering through the breeze

Music of birth
Going forever
Day by day
With the music of a river

Life Before Year 2000

Life is like research
People like scientists
Some of us
Like experimental animals
Jumping on fallen trees

Some of us professors
Others like technicians
All together running
For discovery delicious.

Mistakes and success
In every single lab
Mind in arrest,
Life is like a drug.
The more you experience
The more you want
Because you are scientist
Acting like James Bond

Y2K

Computer In Space

A bank of information
In galactic space
Is for everybody
But you have to find
Your password
Is this enough?
No! then you need
Some kind of visa
Do you have one?
No. I don't need one
I'm a Citizen of the universe
What kind of language
Is there?
Do you have a translator
For this fancy knowledge?

It's the language of the universe
Transformed in your brain
To pictures that you can explain
I don't believe you
How could this be?
But this is true,
You can try me.
Do you agree
To this tough test
Of course
My answer is yes

01/06/98

Why?

People love people
For many reasons
You didn't give me
A single one
Why do I love you?
Do I know?
So let me find out
I love you
For the beauty
Of your soul
For the ocean
In your eyes
For the secrets
Of your mind
For everything
That you are.

What Can I Give You

Diamonds or cookies
Gold or champagne
What can I give you
To not look vain
What can I give you
To make you happy
The treasure of the earth
Or the treasure of the sky
That you can feel
What it means
To be mine

Angels Do Not Survive

Anxiety the fear of a loss
Real or imagined
No body really knows
This negative feeling
Transform for pain
Which creates ability
For powerful demand
This corrective response
Outward of the pain
Express the energy
That makes you anger
You avoid expression
Of your angry mind
Educated person
Learned how to be polite
Negative energy
Turned against yourself
It's perceived as quilt
How to relieve the guilt?
Unrelieved guilt
Transforms to depression

Depression may kill
The strongest personality
How to melt this feeling?
You try your best
But guilt's still not relieved
You feel just depressed
Then danger became
Inviting to the hell
When you pass this gate
You have to transform
Your angel to the devil
To survive there
To relive the guilt
Then you can come back
The guilt free
As an angel or as a devil?

O! don't worry
For sure as an angel
With experience of the devil
Or as a devil
With the soul of an angel
But don't worry
Not now
Now is time
To think how to survive.

Nothing Is Crazy

"Dreams are often most profound when
they seem the most crazy."
- Sigmund Freud

That's crazy, nothing is crazy
It's normal, nothing is normal
It's average, who cares about average
It's physiology, no it's pathology
No it's pathological physiology
No – I disagree
It's physiological pathology
Ok you are right
Because I simply do not argue
But still it doesn't matter
Because nothing is crazy
And nothing is more normal
Than your craziness

Nashville, TN 12.08.07

Forbidden

Don't tell me one more time
You're forbidden one
Because I don't know
What else can I do

Perhaps I can stop
The earth from going round
Or make the full moon fall down

Or make snowflake
Loose it's sixth arm
When my heart
Will break apart

Perhaps I can do it!
But don't try me

Miracle

She came, he felt
She looked, he melt
She smiled, he grew
She touched, he started
She opposed, he won
They danced all night
She fell in love, he lost

A Realist

There was a full moon last night
The same feeling again
A sense of unreality
It's a bit of a difficulty
I'm such a realist
But how can anything
Be real without you?
Why don't you come?
Why don't you come to me....
My dear?

Hopeless

No one to reach this feeling
No one in the whole world
Perhaps I could try the first one
Perhaps he is alright
He sometimes gives me this touch
What about the others?
The others are hopeless
Only using words, no feelings
But the first one . . .
Perhaps . . . .
But how?
He seems to not remember
He's always in a hurry
He never has time

I Do

I love this woman
I used to love her more
Her beauty and her mind
I really loved her more then anything
So what about now?
Do I still love her, do I?
Of course I do, No this is not true
I don't, No this is not possible
How I can't I don't really know
But how can't I know? It's not like me.
I always know, what it means to love
I wish to love her like before
I really wish, with passion of old days
To touch her beauty
With butterflies in my stomach
But I can't, I can't love her.
…What did I said? I hope no body heard,
No body,
I don't want to hear as well.
But… I can't love her,
I don't know how! I really don't.
26.05.98

Erotic Dream

Erotic dream,
Wake me up,
In the middle of life.
I wish to touch you,
And enjoy your soul,
Feel the power.
The power of the dream
That woke me up tonight,
For the rest of my life.
31.07.98

Rock me

Roll, roll, roll my time
Rolling, it's not a crime.
Roll it like it's just paper,
Or like a Rolling Stone.
Roll all the stars within the sky
Roll and don't ask why.
04.06.98

Midlife Crises

"The purpose of poetry is to remind us how
difficult it is to remain just one person."
- Czeslaw Milosz, Nobel Price Laureate

A Full Moon
And a full heart
In full debate
To fool your mind.
Going on a foolish date
At the edge of love -
To find the meaning
Of a distant star.
Is this a fool's existence
In the middle of life,
Or the moon's influence
In the midst of night?

06.06.98

Spoil Me

"The best thing to hold onto
in life is each other."
- Audrey Hepburn

Feed me with the passion of your mind,
Treat me with a soul that is kind.
Touch me with poems of your dream,
Keep me in your hands and between.
Spoil me with your love,
Spoil me or at least try.
04.03.98

Sometimes

"The only reason for time is so that
everything doesn't happen at once."
Albert Einstein

Sometimes feelings are deeper than words.
Sometimes rain is in sunshine.
Sometimes even the sky is empty
Like your mind when it eludes the pain.
Sometimes music is only the background
For your voice of powerful belief.
Sometimes hopeless is each kiss.
Sometimes one touch means too much.
Sometimes it's not possible
To find one person in a big crowd.
Sometimes an empty room is full of love,
When you have just one heart
That is running together with yours.
Sometimes open gates have no doors.
Sometimes it's not possible to sleep
When danger is coming from your own dreams.

Sometimes time means nothing
But sometimes a second may save a life.
Sometimes the sunrise doesn't arrive.
Sometimes nothing happens even if you try.
There is no time for regret, tears to cry.
Many times you depart to come back
But in one instance of departure
...........No return
29.05.98

Would You Hear?

"Joy is a net of love by which
you can catch souls."
- Mother Teresa

No mommy, no daddy
Just me, with open eyes.
With unuseful knowledge
With an open heart and blooming mind.
Just me, in my prime.
Someone loved me before -
Someone will love me later,
But now only dreams
Remind me how love felt
No mommy, no daddy
No lover… only me.
Out of light… only dreams.
Out of dark… only love.
Love didn't find me tonight.
Can I scream… I am here
Can I scream… would you hear…

24.10.03

Between Dark and Dusk

"Art washes away from the soul the
dust of everyday life."
- Pablo Picasso

I yearn to open your soul
With diamonds within my heart
But I cannot find a single door.
Each day keeps us apart.

I cannot touch,
But I can feel.
You think I am nuts
That I don't live in what is real

Forbidden games
On silent nights
Unwritten poems
Are sending lights

Between dark and dusk
With blooming stars
On open sky
Behind lighting's dark

Back to the future
Search with your mind
Don't speak like a butcher
Pleeeaase, just be kind

Reflection will come
Only fill me with pleasure
Touch me with your flame
Then I will open my soul as a treasure

Then you will find who I am

Soul Full Of Flowers

"Everywhere I go I find that a poet
has been there before me."
- Sigmund Freud

A garden full of flowers
A symbol of nature

Flowers full of rainbows
A symbol of beauty

Symbols occupy our minds
Unconsciously in our garden

Reaching our souls,

A soul like a flower enriches the garden
To keep these flowers blooming

To let them simply grow
In the garden,…in your soul

A Plethora Of Poems

"All bad poetry springs from
genuine feeling."

- Oscar Wilde

I have written many poems
Many different kinds
But I never wanted to write
Everything about my mind
I always tried to write
Only one poem
But I always failed
Still unpainted in my mind
Unbelievably beautiful,
Almost perfect
Every time I try, I miss it,
I write something else
I'm too weak to stop trying
Hence the great number of poems
Each of them a different kind of failure

The Notebook

"Everything you can imagine is real."
Pablo Picasso

The excitement in her eyes caught my attention,
What could be so exiting about a notebook
with empty pages, for a little girl

She touched this notebook
And embraced it to her heart,
Like a bible with the secrets of life

A smile on her face convinced me
That her imagination filled all the pages at once
with stories of her mysterious soul
that had never been opened to anybody,
Until now

SHE FOUND A REAL FRIEND
That she can share her thoughts with,
Her disappointments
Her happiness and her sadness

The friend that can listen, accept and understand
her BIG misery
as a little human being

Her THANK YOU was bigger than the mystery
inside

She said nothing else and started to write
With a joy in her eyes,
like a child on her favorite ride

I never thought that an empty notebook
Could be a little girl's most cherished treasure

Nashville, TN 2008

Portrait of Stella Nowicki painted by her Husband

Stella and Bogdan Nowicki

Stella Nowicki medical school graduation photo

My 2 daughters Natalie(left) and Joanna(right bottom) My son Alex(middle), my husband Bogdan(Back), my granddaughter Isabelle(in joanna's arms), and me(right)

Stella at home

Isabelle

Joanna and Isabelle

Natalie Alex Joanna Christmas Picture

Stella and Bogdan Dancing

Stella in the Lab

About the Author

Doctor Stella Nowicki is an amazing woman, and proof that you can have it all. She is currently a Professor of Microbiology and Immunology at Meharry Medical College (MMC), a nationally and internationally recognized scientist, mentor, leader, poet, painter, ballroom dancer, and a fantastic cook, all while being a loving and supportive wife, and mother of 3.

Dr. Nowicki was born and raised in Poland, where she fell inlove with her husband as they danced. She earned her doctoral degree from the Medical University of Gdansk in Poland, and had her first daughter there. The author's ambitions drove her to finish 3 postdoctoral fellowships, first in oral biology at Helsinki University, Finland, the second in molecular microbiology at Baylor College of Medicine, Houston, Texas and the third in human immunology at the Veteran Hospital affiliated with Baylor College of Medicine in Houston, TX.

Prior to joining the MMC she was the director of an experimental laboratory in the Obstetrics and Gynecology Department and a faculty member of the medical and graduate schools at University of Texas Medical Brunch (UTMB), in Galveston, TX. Her research has been supported by grants from National Institute of Health (NIH). for more than 20 years, and has made many important contributions to the advancement in the field of women's health. Dr. Nowicki holds two USA scientific patents, and served as the first Scientific Director of the Women's Health Research Center at Meharry. Now she is a Director for Collaborations and Partnerships at the Meharry Translational Research Center. Previously She served as the President for The Women's Faculty Association at UTMB.

She is an author of over 200 publications, seven invited book chapters and many scientific abstracts and papers which were presented at scientific conferences.

Stella has a long-standing interest uncovering explanations for the notably higher rate of preterm birth and cardiovascular disease in

African –American women, as compared to Caucasian women. Among her many awards are the prestigious Fannie E. Rippel Foundation Award for The Prevention of Cardiovascular Disease in Women. In 2012 she was awarded membership to the International Women's Leadership Association and in 2014 she was selected as a Guest of Honor for the Polish American Medical Society for her outstanding contributions to science, and was awarded Honorary Membership status.

Over all, Stella is as much a star as her name would imply. The mother of 3 lives, loves, and works with a passion that is only matched by the passion of the man she works with, her husband and partner in life, Dr. Bogdan Nowicki.

Her love of poetry started from a young age. It has evolved from scribbling poems in the corners of school books, to winning poetry contests, and finally, publishing a book of her poetry, where she can share little bits of wisdom, artistry, and herself with the world.